I0408049

Limericks on Nature

Written especially for the Young Minds & Nature Enthusiasts

Sanyam Sadana

Printed in the United States

Copyright © 2017 Sanyam Sadana

All Rights Reserved

No part of this publication may be reproduced, stored in a
retrieval system, or transmitted, in any form or by any means,
electronic, mechanical, photocopying, recording or otherwise,
without the prior permission of the author.

Dedication

Dedicated to the lotus feet of Guruji, God, my parents, and the society of which I am an integral part.

TABLE OF CONTENT:

PART 2:

• Articles on Saving the Nature-

About the Author

Sanyam Sadana is a young fiction writer born on 24 September 2000. Although he is Indian by decent, his stories are in a great way influenced by the West. Sanyam Sadana began writing at a very young age, merely ten, and completed his first novel at the age of twelve, an adventure novel for young minds, titled "The Adventures of Dennis Bonaparte", which he later self published. Having written a wide variety of novels and short stories on different genres, Sanyam's interest in poetry made him wrote a large number of poems, ballads and limericks. The author writes his stories in both first as well as third person. He is said to write in an Indian tone, with Western taste. He had his first work published at sixteen, a short novel pointing the evils of caste-system, discrimination and inequality in the society, titled

"Seezerfield", and now continues to write even more interesting stories. After acknowledging himself with the taste of the readers, he wrote his first suspense thriller, "The Mad Man's Dream: A Game of Horror". His work is always full of sarcasm and satire towards the evils of the society which he generally points out in his stories. He has also written several nonfictions, including "A Brain worth Million Dollars" which contains twenty six biographies of poor born millionaires, and an action plan to become rich! A socially active guy, Sanyam Sadana is one of the popular self-published authors and can be easily found online on social sites and discussion panels. His Amazon Author Page is http://amazon.com/author/sanyamsadana. All of his books, biography and other updates can be found here. This book itself is a result of the author's deep connection with nature and is a must-read vivid collection of limericks, articles, a play and a short story all on the theme of nature and its conservation.

A Note to the Reader:

The word 'Nature' is used for the things that are not made by humans. "Nature", in the broadest sense, means the physical world as a whole.

From one point of view, human beings are a prime example of nature, and they interact with its other elements on a constant basis.

From the other point of view, human beings are in conflict with the nature and its elements. They take from nature what they need, without giving back anything.

It is our sole duty to interact with nature on a constant basis, and return the same amount to it that we took from it. In other words, if we cut a tree for obtaining timber, we should in return plant two trees, to maintain the balance.

This book that you are holding in your hands is nothing but a small attempt to motivate the readers to maintain the ecological balance, which is highly disturbed today.

Nature enthusiasts would surely admire this work. Young children should be encouraged by their parents and schools to read such works and participate in environmental activities, so that they could become good human beings in their lives.

Introduction

A limerick is a silly poem with five lines. They are often funny or nonsensical. Limericks were made famous by Edward Lear, a famous author who wrote the "Book of Nonsense" in the 1800's. It was an entire book of silly limericks.

Wikipedia defines it as following:

A limerick is a form of poetry, especially one in five-line, predominantly anapestic meter with a strict rhyme scheme (AABBA), which is sometimes obscene with humorous intent. The first, second and fifth lines are usually longer than the third and fourth.

This Book contains the BEST Limericks written by me on the theme Nature and its elements. Along with 20 limericks, I thought it of utmost importance to add a few articles on the same theme. Readers will find them motivating. Therefore, the book is divided into 2 parts; PART 1 containing the 20 limericks while PART 2 containing the motivating articles. Before ending, I also added a play and a short story on the evils man created and man's behavior towards animals. Thus, this book, titled "Limericks on Nature", is actually a grand collection of short poems called limericks, articles on saving the nature as well as a play and a short story on the same theme. Children should be encouraged to read such works.

PART 1

Limericks

Trees

Trees are here, trees are there,

Different trees are everywhere,

Up they look, in the sky,

None can reach them, they are so

high!

Neither one, nor two, many trees are

everywhere!

Birds

Different shy birds like sparrows and

geese,

But some are there, not like these,

Birds like Penguins, who cannot fly,

In the air, like other birds, so high.

Just say to the birds, don't be shy,

please!

Saving Trees

Trees help in saving the nature

They give oxygen, help in agriculture.

Without trees, man is poor,

Just try to save them, never be

coward,

As trees are important parts of

nature!

Sky

The color of the sky seems to be blue,

Believe it or not, it is true!

Kites and birds, flying so high,

Under the huge blue sky,

Due to earth's atmosphere, the sky

seems blue!

Sun

Sun shines brightly during the day,

Mainly in the months of June and

May,

Eight planets are around the sun,

But our earth is the unique one,

Keep shining, oh sun, let us pray!

Global Warming

Save the earth from global warming,

It is the ozone layer's warning!

Pollution is its main reason,

Its effects are change in season,

Due to heat, the earth is over-

powering!

Milky Way

The Milky Way contains many stars,

They seem to be near, but are very

far!

All the stars, belong to this galaxy,

We can't reach there by car or taxi!

Milky Way galaxy contains thousands

of stars!

Air

Around our earth is a thin layer,

This consists of all the air!

A big part consists of nitrogen,

Rest contains other gases and oxygen,

Together they form the atmosphere!

Freedom

Freedom is the right of all living

things,

The feeling of independence, it brings!

No one is happy being a slave,

Freedom is the fruit of being bold and

brave,

Animals also want it, not only human

beings!

Water

Water is essential for all forms of life,

Either children, or husband or wife,

No one can stay alive without water,

Neither your son, nor your daughter!

So let's save water to save life!

Nature is the one, nature is great!

The power of Creator, it can narrate!

Nature is everywhere, in the form of

trees,

Either butterflies or honeybees!

Technology is responsible for its

decreasing rate!

Stars

A star in the night sky looking so
bright,
It does not reflect but emits its own
light,
It is not near, but very very far,
That's why it looks a very little star,
But we can see it only in night!

Life

Man invented the gun, sword and

knife,

To kill his fellows, to take their life,

But he does not have the right,

To kill others or even to fight,

Thank the Lord for giving us this

precious life!

Pollution

Have we any solution,

Of this increasing pollution?

This is a disease,

Of which earth is to be released,

Let's take an oath to eradicate this evil

pollution!

Water Cycle

Sun dries water during evaporation,

Clouds are formed by condensation,

Rain falls on the ground,

The cycle goes round and round,

Till the next precipitation!

Rainbow

There it is in front of my eyes,

The sun behind me rise,

And a huge colorful arch,

Sees the sparrow, sees the lark,

Far away, but still of great size!

Snow

Soft and white the cool snow,

Falls whereas the breeze do blow,

It is so wonderful and pretty,

That I, sitting next to the settee,

Watch it fall, the chilling snow!

Child

A child is a gift of nature,

God in disguise, till he becomes

mature,

Surrounded by evils, an innocent soul,

Like diamond in a mine of coal,

Pure and innocent is his nature!

Man

A man is really a silly creature,

Who is in the venture to conquer

nature,

He disturbs nature's elements,

Pollutes the environment and tends,

To complete his silly venture!

God

The one who created the nature,

The world with its many creatures,

He is the Ultimate Creator called God,

No one can conquer the power of the

Lord,

We do hurt Him when we disturb the

Nature!

PART 2

Articles on Nature Conservation

Besides limericks, I thought it as a part of my duty to enrich your knowledge about some elements of nature in the form of facts and figures. We hope you will surely help us in our venture to save nature by doing what you ought to do- CONSERVATION OF NATURE!

Below you will find great articles and a play and a short story, as listed below:

• Articles on Saving the Nature-

I. Why to Save the Planet?

II. How to Save the Planet?

III. Global Warming

IV. Water – A Wonder Liquid

V. Conserving Water

VI. Pollution

Before the end of this book, you will also find a play and a story on nature conservation.

 PLAY: The Earth's Disease

SHORT STORY: Animals Day

I.   Why to Save the Planet?

Everywhere around us, nowadays, we hear about SAVING THE NATURE. But do you actually know what the need to save it is?

In this section of this book, you will find the reasons to save the nature, and the ways by which we can practically save it.

To live and let others live, we need to save Mother Earth.

As we all know, our planet is the only one that sustains life, due to various factors like appropriate distance from the Sun and presence of water in all the three states, that are, namely, solid (ice), liquid (water) and gas (steam).

So we really need to save our planet and its never-ending diversity in ecological, biological, cultural as well as environmental issues. But in real life, we are polluting our environment rather than saving it. But, on the other hand, we are doing our part in saving the environment by our daily activities in one way or the other. In this part of my book, I try to deal with various ways that we can adopt to save

Mother Earth and its resources.

II.   How to Save the Planet?

There are many things that we could do to help the environment. We need to help the environment because we live on earth, and this is the only place we can live on right now. If we treat it like the city dump it becomes dirty and unlivable. If we treat it well, the earth stays a clean place, perfect for living, for ourselves and our children. In order to save the environment you need to be aware of what you are doing, buying, using, and what it does to the environment.

Below are given some beautiful articles which inclde tips about saving the planet.

There are many ways we can help save the environment every day. You can reduce the amount of waste you produce by buying products in bulk, rather than in individually wrapped containers. You can also reuse things. Do not throw away unwanted used computer paper, use the other side for scratch paper, and then recycle it. Before you throw broken things away, see how much it would take to repair them. Donate used clothes, furniture, toys, books, and magazines to charity. It is also very easy to recycle. You can try to find recycling centers in your area that will accept toner cartridges, aluminum & steel cans, newspapers & phone books, plastic jugs & bottles, glass jars & bottles, shopping bags, car batteries, and motor oil. Another thing you can do if you have a yard to do it in is compost. Compost makes a great fertilizer for your plants. If you try to stay away from using disposable plates, cups, napkins, and plastic ware, that would help.

Without the Earth we have nowhere to live, along with many other organisms. If we don't save the Earth now maybe our children or grandchildren might not be able to see it for long. Our atmosphere is weakening and we have to do something about it fast.

We could plant more trees to create more oxygen to keep the bad air away from the atmosphere, or we could just stop cutting down the rainforest. We are living and we need the space but we aren't the only species on this earth. Saving the rainforest is not only good for us and the atmosphere but also good for the many different species that it homes.

We could try to get as many people as possible to switch to hybrids and other energy saving things to use less fossil fuel for energy and relying more on solar and wind energy. Fossil fuels are destroying our earth and we need to limit the use of it.

Recycling is a great and easy way to help our precious planet. Everyone can help, all they have to do is follow three simple rules; Reduce, Reuse, Recycle!

The world is precious and we need to keep it that way.

III. Global Warming

Global warming is the term used to describe a gradual increase in the average temperature of the Earth's atmosphere and its oceans, a change that is believed to be permanently changing the Earth's climate. There is great debate among many people, and sometimes in the news, on whether global warming is real (some call it a hoax). But climate scientists looking at the data and facts agree the planet is warming. While many view the effects of global warming to be more substantial and more rapidly occurring than others do, the scientific consensus on climatic changes related to global warming is that the average temperature of the Earth has risen between 0.4 and 0.8 °C over the past 100 years. The increased volumes of carbon dioxide and other greenhouse gases released by the burning of fossil fuels, land clearing, agriculture, and other human activities, are believed to be the primary sources of the global warming that has occurred over the past 50 years. Scientists from the

Intergovernmental Panel on Climate carrying out global warming research have recently predicted that average global temperatures could increase between 1.4 and 5.8 °C by the year 2100. Changes resulting from global warming may include rising sea levels due to the melting of the polar ice caps, as well as an increase in occurrence and severity of storms and other severe weather events.

Throughout its long history, Earth has warmed and cooled time and again. Climate has changed when the planet received more or less sunlight due to subtle shifts in its orbit, as the

atmosphere or surface changed, or

when the Sun's energy varied. But in

the past century, another force has

started to influence Earth's climate:

humanity

How does this warming compare to

previous changes in Earth's climate?

How can we be certain that human-

released greenhouse gases are

causing the warming? How much

more will the Earth warm? How will

Earth respond? Answering these

questions is perhaps the most

significant scientific challenge of our time.

IV. Water: A Wonder Liquid

Water (chemical formula: H_2O) is a transparent fluid which forms the world's streams, lakes, oceans and rain, and is the major constituent of the fluids of living things. As a chemical compound, a water molecule contains one oxygen and two hydrogen atoms that are connected by covalent bonds. Water is a liquid at standard ambient temperature and pressure, but it often co-exists on Earth with its solid state, ice; and gaseous state, steam (water vapor). It also exists as snow, fog, dew and cloud.

Water covers 71% of the Earth's surface. It is vital for all known forms of life. On Earth, 96.5% of the planet's water is found in seas and oceans, 1.7% in groundwater, 1.7% in glaciers and the ice caps of Antarctica and Greenland, a small fraction in other large water bodies, and 0.001% in the air as vapor, clouds (formed of ice and liquid water suspended in air), and precipitation. Only 2.5% of the Earth's water is fresh water, and 98.8% of that water is in ice (excepting ice in clouds) and groundwater. Less than 0.3% of all freshwater is in rivers, lakes, and the atmosphere, and an even smaller amount of the Earth's freshwater (0.003%) is contained within biological bodies and manufactured products.

Water on Earth moves continually through the water cycle of evaporation and transpiration (evapotranspiration), condensation, precipitation, and runoff, usually reaching the sea. Evaporation and transpiration contribute to the precipitation over land. Water used in the production of a good or service is known as virtual water.

Safe drinking water is essential to humans and other life forms even though it provides no calories or organic nutrients. Access to safe drinking water has improved over the last decades in almost every part of the world, but approximately one billion people still lack access to safe water and over 2.5 billion lack access to adequate sanitation. There is a clear correlation between access to safe water and gross domestic product per capita. However, some observers have estimated that by 2025 more than half of the world population will be facing water-based vulnerability. A report, issued in November 2009, suggests that by 2030, in some developing regions of the world, water demand will exceed supply by 50%. Water plays an important role in the world economy, as it functions as a solvent for a wide variety of chemical substances and facilitates industrial cooling and transportation. Approximately 70% of the freshwater used by humans goes to agriculture.

With two thirds of the earth's surface covered by water and the human body consisting of 75 percent of it, it is evidently clear that water is one of the prime elements responsible for life on earth. Water circulates through the land just as it does through the human body, transporting, dissolving, and replenishing nutrients and organic matter, while carrying away waste material. Further in the body, it regulates the activities of fluids, tissues, cells, lymph, blood and glandular secretions.

An average adult body contains 42 liters of water and with just a small loss of 2.7 liters he or she can suffer from dehydration, displaying symptoms of irritability, fatigue, nervousness, dizziness, weakness, headaches and consequently reach a state of pathology. Dr F. Batmanghelidj, in his book 'your body's many cries for water', gives a wonderful essay on water and its vital role in the health of a water 'starved' society. He writes: "Since the 'water' we drink provides for cell function and its volume requirements, the decrease in our daily water intake affects the efficiency of cell activity........as a result chronic dehydration causes symptoms that equal disease..."

Water as a Transporter: Once a substance is dissolved in water, water becomes very important for transporting it throughout the body. Blood, which is 83 percent water, transports oxygen, CO_2, nutrients, waste products, and more from cell to cell. Urine is also mostly water. It is impossible for us to live without water! You can go weeks without food but only 5-7 days without water.

When the water in your body is reduced by just 1 percent, you become thirsty. At 5 percent, muscle strength and endurance declines significantly and you become hot and tired. When the loss reaches 10 percent, delirium and blurred vision occur. A 20 percent reduction results in death. Then why are we wasting such a vital resource? There is an urgent need to conserve it.

V.   Conserving Water

Water water everywhere,

And all the boards did sink.

Water water everywhere,

Nor any drop to drink!

These lines, from *Rhyme of the Ancient Mariner,* are some immemorial, evergreen poetic lines ever written on the theme of conservation of water! Through the poem itself is written on a different theme, these lines depict the plight of a crew of mariners suffering from hunger and thirst in a lonely sea after a storm that ruined their lives! Such is the power of water!

Consider a leaking tap which drops one drop of water in every 3 seconds. How many drops will it waste in 30 seconds? 10! So the number of drops wasted in 60 seconds, i.e. 1 minute, is 20! How many drops are going to be wasted in 60 minutes? The answer is 20×60=1200. So the rate of wasting water is 1200 drops per hour! Do you know how many drops are there in a liter? A liter has 12,174 drops. That means this tap will waste about 1 liter of water in 10 hours!

A drop of water is worth more than a sack of gold to a thirsty man.

We never know the worth of water till the well is dry.

Try imagining a day in your own house without this wonder liquid, and you will understand its worth! Water is our future- it's time to save it! We have not inherited this world from our forefathers; we have borrowed it from our children. Where will our future generations go if we wasted all the water?

Below are some tips to keep in mind while doing everyday chores:

1. Never put water down the drain when there may be another use for it such as watering a plant or garden, or cleaning.

2. Verify that your home is leak-free, because many homes have hidden water leaks. Read your water meter before and after a two-hour period when no water is being used. If the meter does not read exactly the same, there is a leak.

3. Repair dripping faucets by replacing washers. If your faucet is dripping at

the rate of one drop per second, you can expect to waste 2,700 gallons per year which will add to the cost of water and sewer utilities, or strain your septic system.

4. Check for toilet tank leaks by adding food coloring to the tank. If the toilet is leaking, color will appear within 30 minutes. Check the toilet for worn out, corroded or bent parts. Most replacement parts are inexpensive, readily available and easily installed. (Flush as soon as test is done, since food coloring may stain tank.)

5. Avoid flushing the toilet unnecessarily. Dispose of tissues, insects and other such waste in the trash rather than the toilet.

6. Take shorter showers. Replace you showerhead with an ultra-low-flow version. Some units are available that allow you to cut off the flow without adjusting the water temperature knobs.

7. Use the minimum amount of water needed for a bath by closing the drain first and filling the tub only 1/3 full. Stopper tub before turning water. The

initial burst of cold water can be warmed by adding hot water later.

8. Don't let water run while shaving or washing your face. Brush your teeth first while waiting for water to get hot, then wash or shave after filling the basin.

9. Retrofit all wasteful household faucets by installing aerators with flow restrictors.

10. Operate automatic dishwashers and clothes washers only when they are fully loaded or properly set the water level for the size of load you are using.

11. When washing dishes by hand, fill one sink or basin with soapy water. Quickly rinse under a slow-moving stream from the faucet.

12. Store drinking water in the refrigerator rather than letting the tap run every time you want a cool glass of water.

13. Do not use running water to thaw meat or other frozen foods. Defrost food overnight in the refrigerator or by using the defrost setting on your microwave.

14. Kitchen sink disposals require lots of water to operate properly. Start a

compost pile as an alternate method of disposing food waste instead of using a garbage disposal. Garbage disposals also can add 50% to the volume of solids in a septic tank which can lead to malfunctions and maintenance problems.

15. Consider installing an instant water heater on your kitchen sink so you don't have to let the water run while it heats up. This will reduce heating costs for your household.

16. Insulate your water pipes. You'll get hot water faster plus avoid wasting water while it heats up.

17. Never install a water-to-air heat pump or air-conditioning system. Air-to-air models are just as efficient and do not waste water.

18. Install water softening systems only when necessary. Save water and salt by running the minimum amount of regenerations necessary to maintain water softness. Turn softeners off while on vacation.

19. Check your pump. If you have a well at your home, listen to see if the pump kicks on and off while the water is not in use. If it does, you have a leak.

20. When adjusting water temperatures, instead of turning water flow up, try turning it down. If the water is too hot or cold, turn the offender down rather than increasing water flow to balance the temperatures.

So next time you will waste even a single drop, this article would flash in your mind and probably help you out in saving water!

VI. Pollution

Wikipedia defines pollution as the introduction of contaminants into the natural environment that causes adverse change. Pollution can take the form of chemical substances or energy, such as noise, heat or light. Pollutants, the components
of pollution, can be either foreign substances/energies or naturally occurring contaminants.
Look at any ecosystem and there could be multiple forms of contamination—streams full of toxic

chemicals from industrial processes, rivers overloaded with nutrients from farms, trash blowing away from landfills, city skies covered in smog. Even landscapes that appear pristine can experience the effects of pollution sources located hundreds or thousands of miles away.

Pollution may muddy landscapes, poison soils and waterways, or kill plants and animals. Humans are also regularly harmed by pollution. Long-term exposure to air pollution, for example, can lead to chronic respiratory disease, lung cancer and other diseases. Toxic chemicals that accumulate in top predators can make some species unsafe to eat. More than one billion people lack access to clean water and 2.4 billion don't have adequate sanitation, putting them at risk of contracting deadly diseases.

OCEAN LITTER:

Litter in the world's oceans comes from many sources, including containers that fall off ships during storms, trash that washes off city streets into rivers that lead into the sea, and waste from landfills that blows into streams or directly into the ocean. Once in the ocean, this debris may degrade slowly and persist for years, traveling the currents, accumulating in large patches and washing up on beaches.

PESTICIDES AND FERTILIZERS:

Use of pesticides and fertilizers on farms has increased by 26-fold over the past 50 years, fueling increases in crop production globally. But there have been serious environmental consequences. Indiscriminate pesticide and fertilizer application may pollute nearby land and water, and chemicals may wash into nearby streams, waterways and groundwater when it rains. Pesticides can kill non-target organisms, including beneficial insects, soil bacteria and fish.

Fertilizers are not directly toxic, but their presence can alter the nutrient system in freshwater and marine areas. This alteration can result in an explosive growth of algae due to excess nutrients. As a result, the water is depleted of dissolved oxygen, and fish and other aquatic life may be killed.

AIR POLLUTION:

Air pollution brings to mind visions of smokestacks billowing black clouds into the sky, but this pollution comes in many forms. The burning of fossil fuels, in both energy plants and vehicles, releases massive amounts of carbon dioxide into the atmosphere, causing climate change. Industrial processes also emit particulate matter, such as sulfur dioxide, carbon monoxide and other noxious gases. Indoor areas can become polluted by emissions from smoking and cooking. Some of these chemicals, when released into the air, contribute to smog and acid rain. Short term exposure to air pollution can irritate the eyes, nose and throat and cause upper respiratory infections, headaches, nausea and allergic reactions. Long-term exposures can lead to chronic respiratory disease, lung cancer, and heart disease. Long-term exposures also can lead to significant climatic changes that can have far reaching negative impacts on food, water and ecosystems.

NOISE AND LIGHT POLLUTION:

Artificial light and noise often drown out natural landscapes. In the Arctic, the sounds of oil and gas explorations are so loud that belugas, bowhead whales and other sea life have had difficulty feeding and breeding. Light pollution disrupts circadian rhythms for both humans and animals alike and may even contribute to the development of cancer. Light pollution also can impact sea turtles. Adult and hatchling sea turtles are drawn toward lights along the beach, thinking they are heading toward the moon. Coastal developments, therefore, are encouraged to turn off their lights or cover them at night.

WATER POLLUTION:

Clean freshwater is an essential ingredient for a healthy human life, but 1.1 billion people lack access to water and 2.4 billion don't have adequate sanitation. Water becomes polluted from toxic substances dumped or washed into streams and waterways and the discharge of sewage and industrial waste. These pollutants come in many forms— organic, inorganic, and even radioactive—and can make life difficult, if not impossible, for humans, animals and other organisms alike.

HARMFUL ALGAL BLOOMS AND DEAD ZONES:

Human activities, especially agriculture, have led to large increases in the levels of nitrogen and phosphorus in the environment. In water, this overabundance of nutrients, a process called eutrophication, can fuel the excessive growth of phytoplankton and algae, which can sometimes have devastating consequences. Harmful algal blooms—blooms of species that produce deadly toxins and sometimes known as "red tides" or "brown tides" for their appearance in the water— can kill fish, marine mammals and seabirds and harm humans. And when the algae and other organisms that had been allowed to bloom because of the nutrient excess eventually die off, bacteria may suck up all the oxygen from the water as the algae decompose. This hypoxia creates a "dead zone" where fish cannot live. More than 400 areas around the world have been identified as experiencing eutrophication and 169 are hypoxic.

ACID RAIN:

When water in the atmosphere mixes with certain chemicals—particularly sulfur dioxide and nitrogen oxides emitted during the burning of fossil fuels—mild acidic compounds are formed. This acid rain can leach toxic aluminum from the soil, which at low levels can stress fish in lakes and streams or, at higher concentrations, kill them outright. Acid rain also weakens trees in forests and contributes to air pollution that can harm humans. Acid rain is the only monster responsible to corrode historical monuments like Taj Mahal in Agra which still attracts visitors from around the world to the land of diversity, India.

OCEAN GARBAGE PATCHES:

Plastics and other marine debris that can float may persist in the oceans for years, traveling the currents. Some of this material accumulates in the centers of ocean gyres, creating great garbage patches. The term "garbage patch" brings to mind floating islands of trash, but little of the debris can be seen on the surface. Garbage patches, instead, are areas where concentrations of flotsam and jetsam, mostly small pieces of plastic, are particularly high. This litter can distribute toxic chemicals throughout the oceans, snag and tear corals, and harm animals if they ingest pieces of plastic or become entangled in the debris.

Play

The Earth's Disease

Characters:

1. God

2. Earth

3. Tree

4. Pollution

5. Man

Scene I

(God, the Ultimate Creator, decides to meet and understand the feelings of Mother Earth)

God- Hello Earth! I just wanted to meet you. So tell me, how are you?

Earth- I am so happy you cared for me! (Coughs) But actually, I am suffering.

God- Suffering! Suffering from what?

Earth- I am suffering from a fatal disease. The disease is killing me initially day by day!

God- What is the disease? I will surely help you out.

Earth- The name of my disease is p... *(coughs)* ...pollution. It is hazardous to me!

God- Ok. I will meet this pollution.

Scene II

(God meets Pollution)

God- Are you Mr. Pollution?

Pollution- Yes. Who the hell are you?

God- I am God, the creator. I want to know why you are disturbing my creation, Earth.

Pollution- This is in my nature.

God- Wait! Who created you? I never created such an evil thing.

Pollution- Your favorite creation, man created me.

God- And what is your cure?

Pollution- You want to destroy me! Why should I tell you my cure? Do I appear so foolish that I will let you destroy me by myself telling you my cure?

God- I will find out myself!

Scene III

(God again meets Earth)

God- You didn't tell me what can remove pollution?

Earth- Trees are the *only* thing that can cure me from this disease.

God- How? Trees have their own respiratory mechanics. How can they eliminate pollution?

Earth- Oh God! Trees use carbon dioxide gas to respire during the day time in the presence of sunlight. It is only during this time when they will use up all this pollution and emit fresh and clean air, mostly oxygen, and therefore, other life forms would flourish and I will become healthy once again.

God- I have to meet the tree now!

Scene IV

(God meets tree)

Tree- Hello God!

God- Hello! I want to know that if you can remove pollution from the Earth's surface, then why don't you?

Tree- I can only eliminate this pollution only when I am present in large numbers. But I am helpless. I cannot do anything when I am alone. They prefer to cut me rather than growing me!

God- Who cuts you?

Tree- Your favorite creation, man!

God- Oh! Man seems to be in favor of pollution! I will have to meet him!

(God leaves)

Scene V

(God meets Man)

God- I have heard a lot of complaints about you, Humans!

Man- Hello God! What have I done?

God- You created an evil that is initially killing you and this Earth!

Man- I respect Mother Earth.

God- You diseased her by creating pollution.

Man- But I have only created things like vehicles and industries which are beneficial to me!

God- These things are leading to pollution, polluting the planet!

Man- I too want to get rid of pollution!

God- You can! Are you forgetting about my eco-friendly creation, trees? Plant trees in large number and you can get rid of pollution!

Man- How foolish I am! Instead of planting them, I was cutting trees. From today, I will try to fulfill my desires by not disturbing the nature.

God- I am happy you understood within time!

Hope you will look after Mother Earth...

The End

Short Story

Animals Day

Disclaimer

This is a work of fiction. Names, characters, businesses, places, events and incidents are either the products of the author's imagination or used in a fictitious manner. Any resemblance to actual persons, living or dead, or actual events is purely coincidental.

'Sonny, the audience wants a new animal. If you won't bring a new creature by the end of this month, I will be forced to close this zoo and start working as a taxidermist', said Mr. Lone, the zoo owner, to the manager Sonny.

'Why as a taxidermist, sir? You want to stuff dead bodies of innocent animals and sell them as showpieces to some extra rich people?' said Sonny, who could not understand what his boss was saying.

'Oh, I said to become a taxidermist because I love animals. Well, why don't you catch the point, Sonny? I was saying that I would be forced to close this zoo if you do not took the pains to bring a new creature by the end of this month', said Mr. Lone.

'If you really love animals, then why do you want to kill them and stuff their bodies? I cannot believe what you just said', said Sonny.

'What you said you can't believe?' asked Mr. Lone.

'That you love animals', replied Sonny, the manager of the zoo owned by Mr. Lone.

'Oh, so do you think *you* love them?' said Mr. Lone sarcastically.

'I am proud to say yes, I do', said Sonny.

'Oh, I see. That is the reason why you are working as a manager of a zoo in which these poor creatures are kept in cages', said Mr. Lone.

'Why, aren't they lucky to be kept in cages? We care for them more than their mothers would have done for them. They do not need to go for hunting, finding food in the depths of the jungles, or look for fresh water rivers. We provide them with enough food and water. This certainly shows that I really love animals', said Sonny.

'Is this what you call love? And giving them just food and water is what you call care? They are also living beings and they need independence', said Mr. Lone.

'If you know all these points, then why are you running this zoo?' said Sonny, now embarrassed at the ongoing argument with his boss.

'I am running this zoo because I love to see animals in front of my own eyes and in front of my audience. I want to make money, serious money, nothing else!' said Mr. Lone, who was also by now embarrassed at this argument with an employee of his.

'Okay, now will you please tell me what do you want, Mr. Lone?' said Sonny, finally wanting to end this argument.

'I have told you twice. I want you to bring a new creature for my audience. They are bored seeing these old beasts. They want something new and fresh, something different', said Mr. Lone.

'So, tell me, which type of animal I should bring', said Sonny.

'Bring something different this time. A beast which is both cute as well as furious', said Mr. Lone in a deep thought.

'I suppose there exists no such animal who is both cute as well as furious', said Sonny.

'I think there is', said Mr. Lone after a minute of thinking deeply. He would not have thought so deeply even if this was his graduation examinations, thought Sonny.

'A lion cub', said Mr. Lone, finally.

'But...' Sonny was frustrated.

'What but?' asked Mr. Lone.

'But isn't it our protocol NOT to bring cubs in this zoo. They are too young to adjust in the cage', said Sonny.

'Are you the biggest fool on earth? What will we do with the protocols when we would have to close this zoo forever? Forget each and every protocol for a moment. Let the rules, terms and conditions go to hell!' said Mr. Lone.

'But a cub is too young to be kept here', said Sonny.

'Why, isn't it better, or rather I must say BEST to bring cubs? See, when we bring old animals, they find it very difficult to adjust in new surroundings.

You must be remembering the elephant, which caused havoc, because he found these new surroundings unsuitable. Do you know why? Because he was used to live in the forest. But when we will bring cubs here, there would be no such problems, because younger ones can easily adjust in new surroundings. Did you understand, you fathead?' said Mr. Lone.

Sonny could not find words to speak. He could not argue again with his boss, or go against him, or else his job would be lost forever. He had no other choice than to agree what his employer says.

Time passed and the month's closing arrived. Sonny, with his animal catcher team, prepared to depart for the forest. This time, the team was extra prepared and fully armed, for they knew that they would be encountering the cub's mother, who would be ready to die for the life of her cub. Lions usually live with their families, so the animal catching team would have to encounter many lions before they could keep hands on a suitable cub.

Well, by a "suitable cub" they mean that the cub should be old enough to be able to survive without its mother, but young enough to hunt or attack anybody.

While they were going towards the forest, Sonny, the manager of Mr. Lone's zoo, was feeling very sorry for the poor cub which they would be taking along with them on their journey back to the zoo. This would be a difficult task, after all. The thought of dealing with a lioness who wants to save her cub fighting bravely with them gave Sonny as well as the whole animal catcher team chills! Jerry, the lead animal catcher, narrated to Sonny a few tales when mother animals fought with their full will with human beings to save their babies.

Sonny himself remembered a tale his elder sister used to narrate to him in his childhood from the book Panchatantra, a vivid collection of fables which were told in ancient India by a priest to inculcate morals in his disciples. It was not a story of a mother animal fighting for her child, but it was a tale about a shepherd.

Once upon a time, a shepherd while grazing his sheep went a little too far in the forest. There he found a little lion cub. Finding the little creature helpless, he took it with him. The cub enjoyed the company of sheep. The cub felt like the sheep were its own family. Time passed and the cub grew into a lion. Living since his childhood in the company of innocent sheep, the lion did not know that he is made by nature for hunting and prey. One day, another lion came to the shepherd's flock, and ran and roared and hunted a sheep! Seeing this, the lion that grew up among sheep came to know his full potential. He did the same, and hunted another sheep. The shepherd could not believe his eyes. He was afraid, he ran towards the town with the rest of his flock. The two lions returned to the forest. The shepherd realized that no one can keep anybody in the dark. Earlier or later, every lion must come to know about his potentials, thought Sonny, as he recalled this tale in his head.

They reached the forest in the evening. Deciding not to go inside in the woods at this time of the day, when the sun was about to set and the predators were about to start their hunting quest, the zoo team decided to spend the night in a cottage situated in the outskirts of the jungle.

Somehow, the night passed. The sun rose from the eastern horizon. Sonny still proposed Jerry, the leader of the animal catching team, that they should return empty handed, as it is not at all right to catch a lion cub.

'Your worries are logical, but we have no choice, or else that stupid zoo owner Mr. Lone will fire us!' said Jerry.

They silently headed towards the jungle after eating a breakfast of tomato and cucumber sandwich, where a fierce encounter with a brave lioness awaited them...

A young cub, named Prince, the son of the King of the forest and the nephew of Leo, the most fierce lion who can scare even a herd of wild buffaloes by his roar, was heading towards the pond with his mother. Prince was just a year old, and his parents and Uncle Leo were planning to teach him how to hunt, as it was very essential for the survival of a lion in a forest.

As Jerry and his team, along with the manager Sonny, reached near the pond, they spotted a cub with his mother drinking water. They quickly settled their equipments there only, thinking that Prince was the most suitable cub for them. He looked old enough to be able to live in the zoo, and young enough to hunt or disturb other animals there in the zoo. Jerry loaded his gun with bullets of anesthesia, which would make anyone unconscious if hit by it.

A trap was kept ready to catch the cub. Jerry aimed his anesthetic gun towards Prince. His mother, the lioness, spotted the gun before it could hit her or her son. She attacked Jerry, who immediately fired a bullet in her abdomen. She was unconscious. Prince stood motionless. That little cub could not understand what was happening, but was sure that these human beings are no good.

Four men jumped with the trap towards Prince, who was immediately caught in the trap. The team moved towards the cottage where their van was waiting for them.

They left the forest and headed towards the zoo in the city.

***

'Oh, what a cute animal you have brought! I think I should give you a bonus today', said Mr. Lone, as he stood amazed at the sight of Prince, the cub, struggling to get rid of the trap he was caught in.

'I thought that I won't return alive when its mother attacked me', said Jerry, remembering the fearful incident.

'But luck is always with me, I mean *us*', said Mr. Lone.

'Should we keep him in the cage?' asked Sonny.

'Why? Why should we keep Jerry in the cage?' asked Mr. Lone, confused and surprised.

'I am talking about this cub', said Sonny.

'Oh, you should have said "it" instead of "him". You rather made me confused. Is this cub a lion?' said Mr. Lone.

'No, it's a cow', replied Jerry.

'You stupid, I mean is this a male lion or a female lioness', said Mr. Lone.

'Yeah, it's male', replied Jerry.

'Good. Go and keep it in the cage. It would be a great centre of attraction', said Mr. Lone.

'With who should it kept?' asked Sonny.

'Ok, do one thing. Keep me with him', said a frustrated Mr. Lone.

'Then who will look after all your money and property?' said Jerry.

'The *langoor* will become my heir', said Mr. Lone.

'Oh, he is an appropriate match!' Jerry laughed as he said this.

'I am not in a mood of cracking jokes and all that. And you, Sonny, why do you want a company for this little beast?' said Mr. Lone.

'He, I mean, *it* is too young to live alone. It won't be able to adjust. We should at least keep any young animal with it', said Sonny.

'Ok. Keep the rhinoceros with it. The rhino is a perfect match for a little lion cub. This cub will learn to be calm in the presence of the rhino', said Mr. Lone.

'Ok', Sonny nodded and left, taking the cub in the trap along with him.

The cub was kept in the cage with the rhinoceros. Prince could not make out what was happening with him. The sight of a rhinoceros gave him pleasure. 'At least, there are other members of the forest here', Prince thought.

The rhino stood quietly in front of this new member. He was curious to talk to a lion cub, and started looking for an appropriate opportunity to do so.

Prince closely examined the iron bars of the cage. He tried to bite them in order to break the cage and escape from this wicked place. The rhino was seeing him from a little distance.

Finally, the rhino said, 'You are trying in vain, dear!'

'I am a brave lion and lions can do anything. We don't try anything in vain. Whatever we try, we do achieve', said Prince, triumphantly.

'Oh, I see', the rhinoceros was admiring the courage of the lion cub.

'Well, will you be my friend?' asked the rhino.

'A horse cannot befriend the grass', Prince replied.

'You are just a cub, and I am not a grass', said the rhino.

'I mean, lions cannot befriend their prey. My uncle told me this', said Prince.

'As far as I know, I haven't seen any lion eating a rhinoceros', said the rhino.

'I think you are right. My uncle never told me any anecdote of his when he hunted a rhinoceros', said Prince.

'So, would you like to be my friend? It is better if you befriend every animal of the zoo. We have to live here for the rest of our lives', said the rhino.

'What is a zoo? And why do we have to live here forever?' asked a terrified Prince.

'A zoo is a place where they display wild animals. They keep us in cages. They take away our freedom. One who comes here never ever returns to the forest', told the rhino.

The thought of staying here forever gave Prince a chill over his spine.

The elephant from the adjacent cage, who overheard their conversation, joined them in the conversation.

'Do you know it is the first time they brought a cub from the jungle? I have heard that it is a protocol of the zoo not to bring baby animals', said the elephant.

'Wow! Would you please describe how you felt when you lost your parents after being caught by these human beings?' said a giraffe who was peeping inside the cage from the fence.

Prince felt delighted as he had never thought of talking to such a variety of animals. They all pleaded him to narrate his feelings when they brought him to the zoo.

Prince narrated to them about the day when he was born.

'My father was very happy when I was born. 'Here comes the next king of the forest! Announce in the whole jungle the arrival of a little prince', he said to my uncle. Thus, I was named Prince. Not only my father or other lions, but whole of the forest was glad on my arrival in the world. Elephants triumphed, monkeys danced and chinkaras ran here and there out of enjoyment. No one, not even my always eager to do so Uncle Leo, went for hunting that day when I was born', he said.

He then told his feelings when the human beings shot his mother and caught him in a trap. During his whole journey from the forest to the zoo, he was thinking why did they caught him and what did they did to his mother.

'They only made your mother temporarily unconscious. She would have been alright within a few hours', said the elephant.

'How do you know this?' asked little Prince.

'You see, I am from India. They did the same with many animals in the dense Indian forests. And they used to ride me on their hunt. They would sit on my back with guns in hands', said the elephant.

'I have heard about India from my father. He told me one day that as Indians fought for their independence, we animals should also fight for our own freedom', said Prince.

'How did the Indians fought for freedom?' asked the giraffe eagerly.

'My father told me that they adopted several peaceful ways to do so. One of them was to celebrate Independence Day even when they were being ruled. This made the colonizers realize that they really need freedom. Their leader, a non-violent peace maker called Gandhi Ji, talked peacefully to the Viceroy and asked them to set the Indians free', said Prince.

'So why don't we try something of that sort?' proposed the rhino.

'What? Should we call Gandhi Ji for our rescue?' asked the elephant.

'But unfortunately, Gandhi Ji is no more alive', said Prince.

'Oh, that man was our last hope', said the giraffe.

'Oh, stop all this! I am not talking about calling Gandhi Ji to our rescue. But I think we should on our own talk to the higher authorities of the zoo', said the rhino.

'How can we talk with them? Our ancestors have told us, or more appropriately I should say warned us, that we should not let the humans know that we can talk', said the elephant.

'Look, the choice is ours. Either we should talk to them, or spend the rest of our lives in cages', said the rhino.

'I think you are right', said Prince to the rhinoceros. 'We will talk to them.'

The animals were sitting quietly and motionless when a zoo worker came to give them food. As soon as the worker kept a piece of meat in front of Prince, the lion cub spoke, 'Will you please call the owner of this zoo. We want to talk to him.'

Suppose you go for watering the plants in your little garden, as you are accustomed to do since many years. But suddenly one day a plant speaks to you! How would you feel? The same was the plight of that worker. Seeing the cub, or more appropriately, hearing the cub, the worker screamed with terror. Without even replying to the lion cub, he ran from the spot.

The worker went straight to Sonny, the manager. Seeing his pale face, Sonny asked, 'What happened? Why are you so afraid? Have you seen a ghost in the zoo?'

'Yes, sir, I saw a ghost', said the worker in a very serious tone.

'What to do mean? This is an animal zoo, not ghost zoo or a haunted cemetery', said Sonny.

'Sir, the new arrival, the lion cub, spoke to me in pure English. He said he wants to talk to the owner of this zoo', said the worker.

'Oh, I know. You want a leave. Ok, go home and take rest. Come tomorrow', said Sonny.

'No, sir, even my wife is not at home today. What would I do at home?' said the worker.

'So go to the bar or restaurant. Do whatever you want to do, but please do not cook stories of speaking cubs. I am myself disappointed at the arrival of a cub. Don't add fuel to fire. Now leave', said an embarrassed Sonny.

'If you don't believe me, come with me to see the truth', said the worker.

'Ok, if you wish, I will come with you', said Sonny.

The manager Sonny went along the worker to the cage in which the lion cub was kept.

Standing in front of the cage, Sonny waited for the cub to say something. The worker said to the cub, 'Here I bring the manager of this zoo.'

Sonny was laughing at the silly acts of the worker when they heard a voice. 'Hello, I just wanted to talk to you for a moment, if you can spare', said a young voice.

Sonny was startled. He looked towards the cub and rubbed his eyes.

'Only if you can spare a few minute', said the cub.

'But...' said a surprised Sonny.

'I was right, sir', said the worker triumphantly.

'I did not know that animals can speak', said Sonny.

'Yeah, our ancestors made this decision to keep quiet in front of human beings' said the elephant.

The manager and the worker were again startled. They glared at the elephant.

'But we had to break that rule in order to seek independence', said the rhino.

'Yes, if you can break the protocol of bringing cubs to the zoo, can't we break the protocol of talking to you?' said the giraffe.

The worker was about to faint. Sonny shook himself as if in a dream and wanting to wake. But nothing happened. This was the reality he was really facing.

'You are not in a dream. This is your problem. You never try to understand the reality', said Prince.

'What do you want?' said Sonny, finally.

'We want freedom, nothing less or nothing more!' exclaimed the elephant.

'See, we fill our stomachs by displaying you animals. People admire you, that's why they are paying just to see you', said Sonny.

'So, why don't you open a museum?' said the giraffe.

'Look at yourself. You are stars, I mean, superstars! There is a large fan following of you people. And we give you shelter, safety, and most of all, food and water. Imagine the struggles you people, I mean, animals; have to face in the forests. Hunters want to shoot you; poachers want your skin, nails, jaws, tusks and other body parts; you have to wander here and there in search of food and water. You should be thankful to us. Can't you just spend your life in cage as a return to what we are giving you?' said Sonny.

The animals stood amazed and speechless at his wonderful speech.

'You cannot keep a bird happy even if you keep it in a cage made up of gold! Now or then, the bird only wants freedom, nothing else!' said Prince, after thinking deeply about the logic given by Sonny.

Sonny had no reply. Finally, he thought of some possible adjustment.

'Listen, it is not possible for us to send you back to the forest. We also have kids and families, and we have to fulfill all the expanses of life. You are our livelihood. But I think I can do something', said Sonny.

'Oh, nothing else would work', said the rhino.

'You see, I am not the owner of this zoo. I am just a manager, an employee of the rich owner named Mr. Lone. Still I can arrange a day of independence for you', said Sonny.

'Wow, would we really be able to celebrate Independence Day? Do you mean you will set us free one day?' asked an eager giraffe.

'Yes and no. I mean that I can arrange to set you free *for* one day. A single day and all of you can do whatever you want to do. It is inappropriate to call this Independence Day, for Independence Day means that you will be set free forever on that particular day. But you see that is not possible. So I can give you a single day of your own, or the *Animals Day*, but you have to promise that the next day, you will peacefully return to the cages', said Sonny.

The animals went in deep thought.

'The idea is not too bad', said the rhino.

'But, we want complete independence. This won't work', said the elephant.

'Listen, I don't see we have another choice', said the giraffe.

'Ok, we agree', said the cub to Sonny.

'Let me first ask the zoo owner for his permission', said Sonny.

'Bring him here, we will ourselves express our feelings to him', said the elephant.

The owner, Mr. Lone was immediately called. Startled at the discovery of talking animals, he immediately agreed to do whatever they want. But it was hard for a businessman like Mr. Lone to agree such a clause. After a brief discussion, and Sonny persuading him to do so, Mr. Lone agreed.

The next day was declared to be the Animals Day. The news spread throughout the zoo. Every beast and bird became excited for the upcoming day. The news soon spread through the city. Someone informed the police and the police arrived at the zoo in the evening.

'You cannot set the wild animals free. They may cause havoc', said the police man.

'But we promise, we will keep them within the zoo premises only. The visitors can see them only from a safe distance. Of course, guards will be present for the visitors' safety', said Sonny.

The police man was convinced.

The night passed and the next morning arrived. The cages were opened. Guards stood at all the borders. Unexpectedly, there was a huge crowd at the ticket counter. Mr. Lone who was viewing the crowd rushed towards it, thinking that some argument is taking place. *But to his pleasant surprise*, PEOPLE WERE BUYING TICKETS! Mr. Lone could see money flowing in his safes!

The cub stepped out of the cage along with the rhinoceros. The elephant crossed the fence. Deer jumped out in the open space and started grazing and running! The entire scene of the so-called zoo was fantastically beautiful and wild! In fact, no animal even tried to hurt the visitors standing at a little distance due to the unexpected overcrowding.

'Why don't they come daily in such huge masses?' asked Mr. Lone to Sonny.

'Maybe they like to see the animals enjoying independence rather than seeing them lying almost dead in the cages behind the iron bars', replied Sonny.

'So why not grant them this freedom forever?' said Mr. Lone.

'Can this really happen?' said a joyful Sonny.

'Yes, I am getting the land behind the zoo for a great price! That land is so much planted that it will appear to be a real forest. And we can arrange for jeeps and buses to take the visitors there. The visitors will surely enjoy the sight of a forest and the independence these animals will be enjoying!' said Mr. Lone.

'This is a great idea', said Sonny.

Arrangements to do so were made immediately. Sonny himself informed about this to the animals, who were very happy at this decision. Finally, the Animals Day proved to be the Independence Day for them.

Prince, the only cub in the zoo, was held responsible for these changes. All the animals thanked him. But little Prince was still longing to go to his own forest, to his own family. Sonny and other animals could see his disappointment, and therefore, Sonny persuaded Mr. Lone to send Prince back.

'You see, Mr. Lone, there is no reason now to break our protocol. The presence of a cub won't affect the crowd coming here', Sonny said to Mr. Lone.

'I think you are right, Sonny. You can send him back', said the zoo owner.

Thus, the cub was sent back after seeing the successful formation of the first *wildlife sanctuary* ever!

The End

www.ingramcontent.com/pod-product-compliance
Lightning Source LLC
Chambersburg PA
CBHW072133280526
45788CB00002B/618